DAVID BECKHAM

MIDFIELD MEGASTAR

PERCY LEED

LERNER PUBLICATIONS ◆ MINNEAPOLIS

Lerner Publications Company
An imprint of Lerner Publishing Group, Inc.
241 First Avenue North
Minneapolis, MN 55401 USA

For reading levels and more information, look up this title at www.lernerbooks.com.

Main body text set in Myriad Pro Semibold. Typeface provided by Adobe.

Library of Congress Cataloging-in-Publication Data

Names: Leed, Percy, 1968– author.
Title: David Beckham : midfield megastar / Percy Leed.
Description: Minneapolis : Lerner Publications, [2022] | Series: Epic sports bios (Lerner sports) | Includes bibliographical references and index. | Audience: Ages 7–11 | Audience: Grades 2–3 | Summary: "David Beckham starred for great soccer teams in England, Spain, and the United States. Off the field, he's one of the biggest superstars in sports. Read about the life of a soccer celebrity" —Provided by publisher.
Identifiers: LCCN 2020046216 (print) | LCCN 2020046217 (ebook) | ISBN 9781728404288 (library binding) | ISBN 9781728420462 (paperback) | ISBN 9781728418063 (ebook)
Subjects: LCSH: Beckham, David, 1975– —Juvenile literature. | Soccer players—England—Biography—Juvenile literature. | Soccer midfielders—England—Biography—Juvenile literature.
Classification: LCC GV942.7.B432 L44 2022 (print) | LCC GV942.7.B432 (ebook) | DDC 796.334092 [B]—dc23

LC record available at https://lccn.loc.gov/2020046216
LC ebook record available at https://lccn.loc.gov/2020046217

Manufactured in the United States of America
1-48486-49000-12/17/2020

TABLE OF CONTENTS

WORLD CUP WINNER

Apenalty kick in a World Cup match is always a big deal. But in the 2002 World Cup, the stakes for David Beckham were even higher. His country, England, was playing its most bitter rival, Argentina.

Beckham takes a penalty kick against Argentina.

FACTS AT A GLANCE

Date of birth: May 2, 1975

Position: midfielder

League: Premier League, La Liga, Major League Soccer (MLS), and Ligue 1

Professional highlights: signed with Manchester United at the age of 11; won the treble with Manchester United; won two MLS titles

Personal highlights: his father was a huge Manchester United fan; has four children; became the highest-paid athlete in the world

Beckham had lived a charmed life. He was only 27 years old, but he'd been a soccer superstar for years. He was a huge part of the Manchester United teams that dominated English soccer at the time. He also starred on England's national team and was even named captain in early 2001. As a team leader, he had to help England beat Argentina.

Beckham wore a yellow armband to show that he was England's captain.

Beckham and his teammates celebrate after beating Argentina.

Beckham's chance came late in the first half of their first-round match. With the score tied 0–0, the referee awarded England a penalty kick. Beckham decided not to try a fancy shot. He'd just bang the ball as hard as he could. "I was far too nervous to try to be clever," he said. Beckham slammed the ball into the middle of the net, past the surprised goalkeeper. The score helped England beat Argentina 1–0!

DREAM COMING TRUE

David Beckham was born on May 2, 1975, in London, England. His father, Ted, installed kitchens and his mother, Sandra, was a hairdresser. David had an older sister, Lynne, and a younger sister, Joanne.

David wears a Manchester United jersey in 1992.

David (*first row, second from left*) poses with members of his youth team.

David spent most of his free time playing soccer. His father was a huge fan of pro team Manchester United. Ted often took David to see them play. By the time David was five, he told everyone that he would play for United someday.

At the age of seven, David began playing organized soccer. He was the star of his team. In three seasons, he scored more than 100 goals. He began to attract serious attention from pro scouts.

The Premier League—the soccer league to which Manchester United belongs—allows young players to join pro teams at any age. When David was about 11, he got a tryout with United. David's skills and hard work made a good impression. United signed him to a contract. "We are delighted that he is joining us," the team announced.

Beckham blows by a Liverpool defender.

Beckham holds the FA Cup trophy after Manchester United won the event in 1996.

David played for Manchester United's youth teams. He competed, day after day, against other talented players. He had great skill with the ball, and he worked hard to succeed. In 1992, he scored a goal to help United win the FA Youth Cup.

In the 1995–1996 season, Beckham began playing full-time for Manchester United's top team. He helped United score one huge goal after another. In his first full season, United won the Premier League and the FA Cup!

Beckham couldn't wait to play in 1996–1997. Manchester United began the Premier League season by beating Wimbledon 3–0. Near the end of the game, Beckham took a long shot. The ball looked as though it was going to go out of bounds, but it curved into the net. Beckham had just scored the most amazing goal of the season.

Beckham keeps the ball away from a Wimbledon defender during the first game of the 1996–1997 Premier League season.

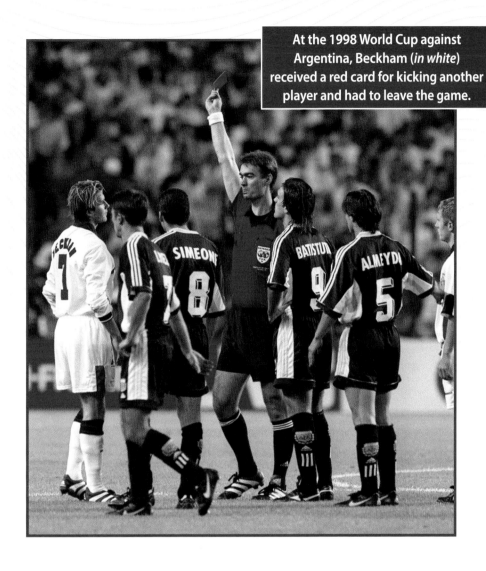

At the 1998 World Cup against Argentina, Beckham (*in white*) received a red card for kicking another player and had to leave the game.

One month later, Beckham was called to represent England for the first time. He helped his national team qualify for the 1998 World Cup in France. The team made it to the knockout round before losing to Argentina in penalty kicks.

A STAR IS MADE

Near the beginning of 1999, United qualified for the Champions League and was in the hunt for the Premier League title. The team also advanced in the FA Cup. No English team had ever won the treble by winning the Premier League, FA Cup, and Champions League in the same season. But in 1999, United had a chance to do it.

Beckham celebrates after scoring a long goal against Arsenal in the 1999 FA Cup. His kick traveled 105 feet (32 m) to reach the net.

CHAMPIONS LEAGUE

The Champions League, originally called the European Cup, began in 1955. The original format allowed only the champion of each nation to participate. It was renamed the Champions League in the 1990s. As many as four teams from a country may enter.

United was within three wins of the treble. The first match, which could clinch the Premier League, was against Tottenham Hotspur. Beckham blasted a shot into the top corner of the net in the first half, and his team won 2–1.

United beat Newcastle 2–0 in the FA Cup final. Normally, winning the Premier League and the FA Cup would have kicked off a big celebration. But the Champions League final against Bayern Munich, a German team, was just four days away. United stayed focused.

Bayern scored after just six minutes, and the German team came close to putting the match out of reach several times. With less than three minutes remaining, Beckham kicked the ball to the front of Bayern's net. The ball bounced to the foot of United's Teddy Sheringham, who poked it in to tie the game.

Two minutes remained, and United kept attacking. Beckham kicked the ball toward Sheringham. Sheringham redirected the ball with his head to Ole Gunnar Solskjaer, who put the ball into the far corner of the net. Goal! United had achieved the treble!

A Bayern Munich defender tries to take the ball away from Beckham during the 1999 Champions League final.

Victoria Adams shows off her engagement ring.

In 1999, Beckham married Victoria Adams of the Spice Girls, a well-known pop group. Only close friends and family members attended the ceremony. More than 340 guests attended the reception. Beckham and his wife were very comfortable being celebrities. They knew full well that their marriage, which many in Britain dubbed the Wedding of the Decade, was bound to make them even more famous.

ENGLAND CAPTAIN

In June 2003, Beckham left Manchester United and joined Spain's Real Madrid, the most successful team in European soccer history. He was sad to leave United, but he was excited for a fresh start in Spain. "To play for Real is a dream come true," he said.

Beckham fights for the ball during his first season with Real Madrid.

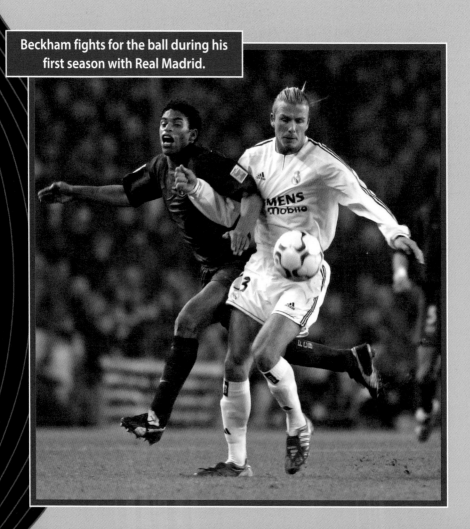

Beckham knew that playing in Spain would be a big change. He took some Spanish language lessons, but he also knew that many of his teammates spoke English and other languages. He was famous in Spain before he even arrived. Real Madrid fans were especially impressed by his hard work and commitment to winning.

Real Madrid started the 2003–2004 season well. Before 2003 ended, the team had advanced in the Champions League and moved into first place in Spain's top league, La Liga. But in April 2004, Monaco eliminated Real from the Champions League. Then Real lost an eight-point lead and finished third behind Valencia and Barcelona in La Liga.

Beckham shaved his head in 2004. Fans and media members closely followed the superstar's changing hairstyles.

Beckham blasts a shot against Portugal at the 2006 World Cup.

Beckham shifted his attention to the international game for the 2006 World Cup. England started out against Paraguay. Paraguay's Carlos Gamarra accidentally headed one of Beckham's kicks into his own net. It was the only goal England scored in a 1–0 victory. The team needed to play much better if they hoped to win the World Cup.

England qualified for the knockout round, where they faced Ecuador. The English players struggled to make passes, but Ecuador wasn't performing any better. In the 60th minute, Beckham blasted a shot into the right-hand corner of the net. It was the only goal of the game in another 1–0 England win.

England faced Portugal in the next match. Both teams were cautious, and neither came close to scoring. England's Wayne Rooney received a red card for stomping on a Portugal player in the second half and was ejected from the game. But still neither team could score.

The match went to penalty kicks, and England lost. Beckham and his teammates gave everything they had, but the team rarely performed well in penalty kicks. Once again, England went home disappointed.

THE END OF
AN ERA

Injuries bothered Beckham throughout the first part of the 2006–2007 season. He also clashed with his coach. But Real Madrid excelled, and in June 2007, Beckham and his teammates won La Liga.

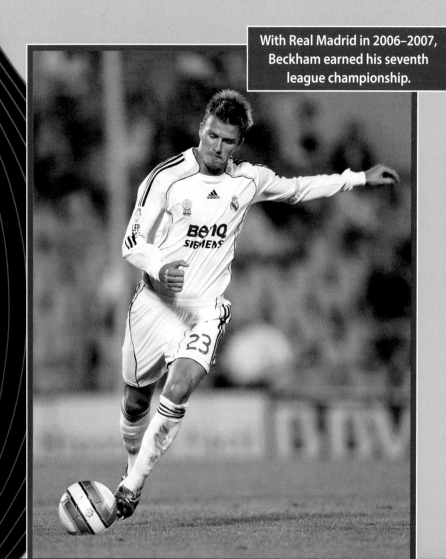

With Real Madrid in 2006–2007, Beckham earned his seventh league championship.

Beckham spends time with kids at an event for the David Beckham Academy in 2005.

Despite winning his first La Liga championship with Real, Beckham was ready for a change. He had long wanted to play soccer in the US. He had already set up his soccer training camp, the David Beckham Academy, outside Los Angeles, California. A life in Los Angeles would help Beckham and his wife pursue careers in the entertainment industry. Few people were surprised when he left Real Madrid after the 2006–2007 season to join the Los Angeles Galaxy of MLS.

Beckham's contract with the Galaxy paid him $250 million over five years. At an average of $50 million per year, the 31-year-old became the highest-paid athlete in the history of team sports at the time. While Beckham was thrilled with the money, he said it wasn't his reason for joining the Galaxy. "This move for me is not about the money," he said. "It's about hopefully making a difference in the [United States] with soccer."

Fans and reporters watched every move Beckham made on the field.

Beckham takes a corner kick during a 2007 game in Los Angeles.

Beckham's signing was the talk of the sports world. MLS, which had trouble gaining headlines in the United States, was front-page news. People who knew next to nothing about soccer were talking about Beckham and MLS.

Beckham spent five seasons with the Galaxy. Playing in his mid-30s, he began to slow down on the field. But he still had the skills that made him an all-time great player. Beckham led the team to back-to-back MLS championships in 2011 and 2012.

Beckham holds up the MLS Cup in 2012 after winning it for the second time with Los Angeles.

In March 2019, David Beckham and Victoria Beckham attended a special event in Los Angeles. The Galaxy revealed a statue of their former star player outside the team's stadium.

After the 2012 season, Beckham left Los Angeles and joined Paris Saint-Germain. In 2013, he helped Paris win Ligue 1, France's top league. In May, he announced his retirement from playing pro soccer. "If you had told me as a young boy I would have played for and won trophies with my boyhood club Manchester United, proudly captained and played for my country over one hundred times, and lined up for some of the biggest clubs in the world, I would have told you it was a fantasy," Beckham said. "I'm fortunate to have realized those dreams."

SIGNIFICANT STATS

Became the first player from England to win pro-league championships in four countries: England, Spain, the United States, and France

Led the Premier League in assists three times

Led MLS in assists per game in 2011

Scored 95 career goals in official pro matches

Recorded 157 career assists in official pro matches

GLOSSARY

contract: an agreement between an athlete and a team that determines a player's salary and time with the team

FA Cup: a large tournament played by pro teams in England

final: a competition's championship game

knockout round: the stage of a tournament in which a game's winning team advances to the next round and the losing team is out of the tournament

penalty kick: a free kick at the goal allowed for certain fouls or to determine the winner of some games

pro: a person who plays a sport for money

red card: a red card that the referee holds in the air to show that a player who has broken the rules must leave the game

treble: a feat achieved by holding three major trophies, including a league title, a national title, and the Champions League title in the same year

tryout: a test of ability

SOURCE NOTES

7   David Beckham, *Beckham: Both Feet on the Ground* (New York: HarperCollins, 2004), 263.

10   Virginia Blackburn, *David Beckham: The Great Betrayal* (London: John Blake, 2003), 23.

18   Beckham, *Beckham*, 366.

24   Jill Serjeant, "Beckham Agreed Los Angeles Move after Advice from Cruise," Reuters, January 21, 2007, https://www.reuters.com /article/us-soccer-beckham-conference/beckham-agreed-los -angeles-move-after-advice-from-cruise-idUSL1200240420070113.

27   Simon Rice, "David Beckham Retires: 'The Time Is Right' to Retire from Football," *Independent* (London), May 16, 2013, https://www .independent.co.uk/sport/football/news/david-beckham-retires -time-right-retire-football-8619336.html.

LEARN MORE

David Beckham
https://www.davidbeckham.com/

David Beckham Biography
https://www.ducksters.com/sports/david_beckham.php

Doeden, Matt. *G.O.A.T. Soccer Teams*. Minneapolis: Lerner Publications, 2021.

Labrecque, Ellen. *Who Is David Beckham?* New York: Penguin Workshop, 2020.

Major League Soccer
https://www.mlssoccer.com/

Savage, Jeff. *Manchester United: Soccer Champions*. Minneapolis: Lerner Publications, 2019.

INDEX

PHOTO ACKNOWLEDGMENTS

Image credits: Mark Pain/Alamy Stock Photo, p. 4; Todd Strand/Independent Picture Service, pp. 5, 28; Aflo Co. Ltd./Alamy Stock Photo, p. 6; AP Photo/Ricardo Mazalan, p. 7; Trinity Mirror/Mirrorpix/Alamy Stock Photo, pp. 8, 9, 11; Sean Dempsey/EMPPL PA Wire/Associated Press, p. 10; REUTERS/Alamy Stock Photo, p. 12; EMPPL PA Wire/Associated Press, pp. 13, 14; AP Photo/Cesar Rangel, p. 16; AP Photo/John Giles, p. 17; AP Photo/Bernat Armangue, pp. 18, 22; AP Photo/Fernando Llano, p. 19; AP Photo/Martin Meissner, p. 20; AP Photo/Stefano Paltera, p. 23; AP Photo/Mark J. Terrill, pp. 24, 25, 26; Sipa USA via AP, p. 27.

Cover: Marty Melville/Getty Images; GIUSEPPE CACACE/AFP/Getty Images (background).